this OR that?
weather

cloud
OR
fog?

Kelly Doudna

Consulting Editor, Diane Craig, M.A./Reading Specialist

Super Sandcastle

An Imprint of Abdo Publishing
abdopublishing.com

abdopublishing.com

Published by Abdo Publishing, a division of ABDO, PO Box 398166, Minneapolis, Minnesota 55439. Copyright © 2016 by Abdo Consulting Group, Inc. International copyrights reserved in all countries. No part of this book may be reproduced in any form without written permission from the publisher. Super SandCastle™ is a trademark and logo of Abdo Publishing.

Printed in the United States of America, North Mankato, Minnesota
102015
012016

Editor: Liz Salzmann
Content Developer: Nancy Tuminelly
Cover and Interior Design and Production: Mighty Media, Inc.
Photo Credits: Kelly Doudna, Shutterstock

Library of Congress Cataloging-in-Publication Data
Doudna, Kelly, 1963- author.
 Cloud or fog? / Kelly Doudna ; consulting editor, Diane Craig.
    pages cm -- (This or that? Weather)
 ISBN 978-1-62403-953-9
1. Clouds--Juvenile literature. 2. Fog--Juvenile literature. I. Craig, Diane, editor. II. Title.
 QC921.35D67 2016
 551.57'6--dc23
                          2015020595

Super SandCastle™ books are created by a team of professional educators, reading specialists, and content developers around five essential components—phonemic awareness, phonics, vocabulary, text comprehension, and fluency—to assist young readers as they develop reading skills and strategies and increase their general knowledge. All books are written, reviewed, and leveled for guided reading and early reading intervention programs for use in shared, guided, and independent reading and writing activities to support a balanced approach to literacy instruction.

contents

cloud or fog?

Is it a cloud? Or is it fog? Do you know the difference?

A cloud is made up of tiny **droplets** of water. They float in the air.

Fog is also made up of tiny **droplets** of water. Fog is a cloud on the ground.

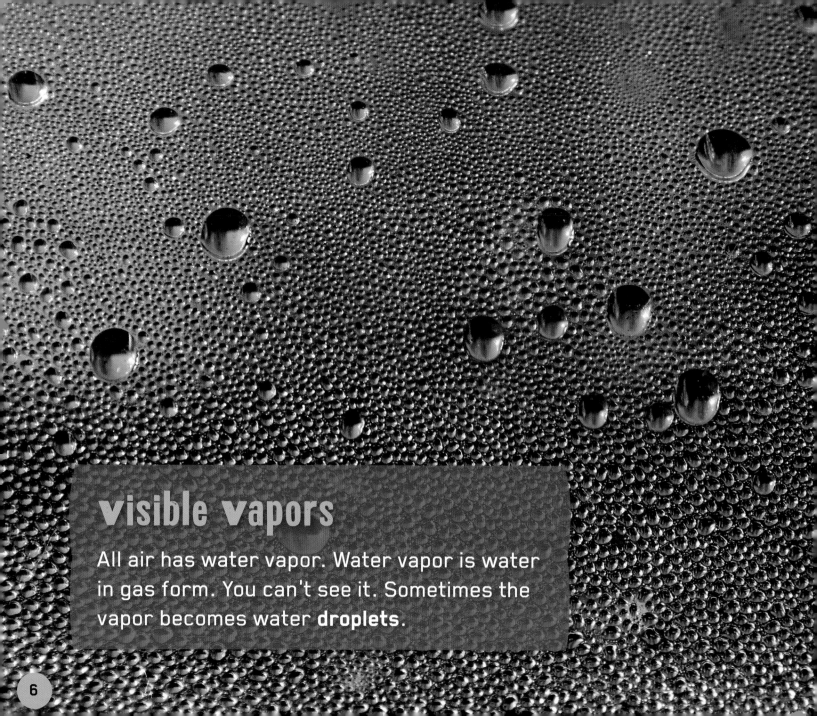

visible vapors

All air has water vapor. Water vapor is water in gas form. You can't see it. Sometimes the vapor becomes water **droplets**.

You can see the water **droplets**. They bunch together. They form clouds and fog.

dust and droplets

The sun warms the air during the day.
The warm air rises. It cools off as it rises.
Cool air can't hold as much water vapor.

Air **contains** tiny bits of dust. Water vapor turns into **droplets** around the dust. The droplets form a group. It gets bigger and bigger. You see a cloud when there are enough droplets.

Fog also happens when water vapor forms **droplets**. Sometimes the air near the ground cools. It becomes too cool to hold the water vapor.

name that cloud!

A cloud's name can have one or two parts. One part tells how high up it is. The other part tells what it looks like.

how high is it?

Cirro means it's a high cloud.
Alto means it's in the middle.
Strato means it's a low cloud.

Cirrus clouds
are **wispy**.

Cumulus clouds
are puffy.

Stratus clouds
are smooth and flat.

Nimbo or *nimbus*
clouds produce rain.

fog formation

Fog is formed in four main ways.

The ground is cooled by night air. The air above the ground cools too. *Radiation fog* forms.

Warmer air moves over cooler land or water. The air cools. *Advection fog* forms.

radiation fog

advection fog

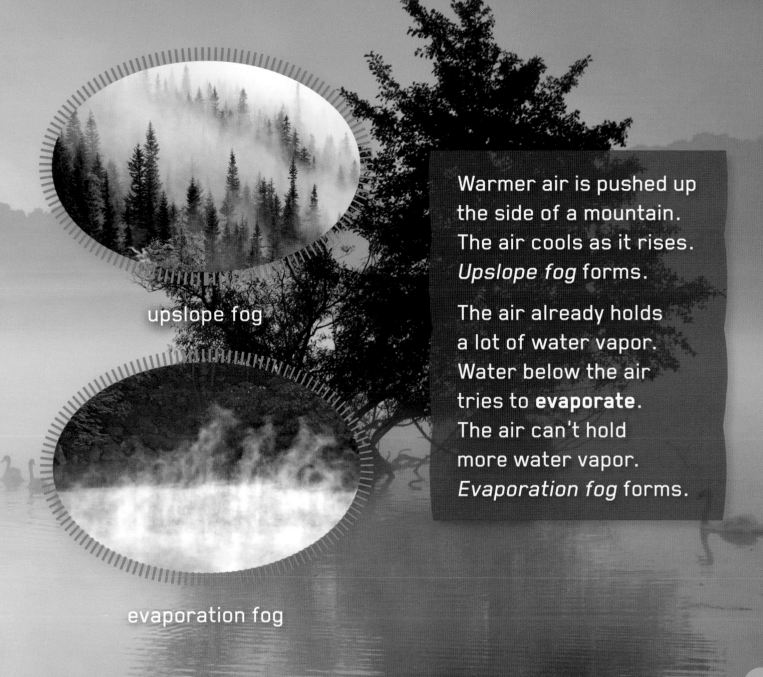

upslope fog

evaporation fog

Warmer air is pushed up the side of a mountain. The air cools as it rises. *Upslope fog* forms.

The air already holds a lot of water vapor. Water below the air tries to **evaporate**. The air can't hold more water vapor. *Evaporation fog* forms.

that's odd

A contrail is a special kind of cloud. It looks like a thin line. Jet airplanes make contrails.

Freezing fog happens in very cold air. The water vapor freezes into tiny ice crystals.

how bad is it?

Storms come from clouds. A thunderstorm is a summer storm. A **blizzard** is a winter storm.

Fog doesn't make storms. But it does make it hard for people to see. This can cause car **accidents**.

here or there?

Clouds form in the sky. This means that they can happen anywhere.

Fog forms near the ground. It needs certain conditions. These conditions aren't everywhere. So fog can't form everywhere.

at a glance

cloud ———————— fog

made up of tiny water **droplets** ——— made up of tiny water droplets

forms in the sky ———————— forms near the ground

four main kinds ———————— four main ways of forming

forms everywhere ——————— forms in places with
around the world certain conditions

can produce storms ———————— makes it hard to see

fog in a bowl

form some fun fog.

What You'll Need
- medium plastic zipper bag
- ice cubes
- measuring cup
- water
- pie plate
- large clear bowl
- matches

1 Fill the plastic bag with ice cubes. Pour 2 cups of warm water into the pie plate. The water should not be hot.

2 Hold the bowl upside down. Hold it a few inches above the pie plate.

3 Have an adult light a match. Blow out the match. Wave the match under the bowl. Lower the bowl onto the pie plate.

4 Lay the bag of ice cubes on the bowl. Wait 1 minute. What happens?

5 Remove the ice cubes. Put your hands on the bowl. Keep them there. Now what happens?

think about it

How did the smoke help to make fog? How did the ice cubes help? What effect did your warm hands have?

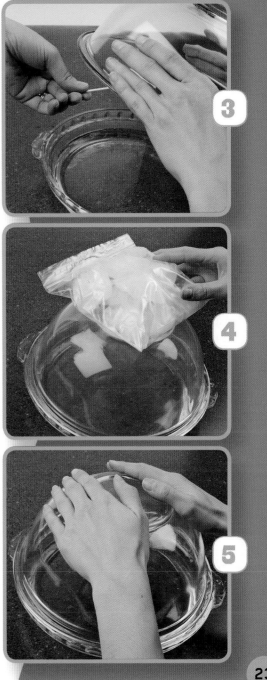

glossary

accident – an unplanned event, often causing harm or damage.

blizzard – a heavy snowstorm with very strong winds.

contain – to consist of or include.

droplet – a very small drop of liquid.

evaporate – to change from a liquid into a gas.

wispy – thin, faint, streaky, or delicate.